"9Marks, as a ministry, has ⌐ ⌐ ⌐ ⌐ irch and put it into
the hands of pastors. Bobby, by way of these study guides, has taken this teaching and
delivered it to the person in the pew. I am unaware of any other tool that so thoroughly
and practically helps Christians understand God's plan for the local church. I can't wait
to use these studies in my own congregation."

Jeramie Rinne, Senior Pastor, South Shore Baptist Church, Hingham,
Massachusetts

"Bobby Jamieson has done local church pastors an incredible service by writing these
study guides. Clear, biblical, and practical, they introduce the biblical basis for a healthy
church. But more importantly, they challenge and equip church members to be part of
the process of improving their own church's health. The studies work for individual,
small group, and larger group settings. I have used them for the last year at my own
church and appreciate how easy they are to adapt to my own setting. I don't know of
anything else like them. Highly recommended!"

Michael Lawrence, Senior Pastor, Hinson Baptist Church, *Biblical Theology in the
Life of the Church*

"This is a Bible study that is actually rooted in the Bible and involves actual study. In
the 9Marks Healthy Church Study Guides series a new standard has been set for personal theological discovery and corresponding personal application. Rich exposition,
compelling questions, and clear syntheses combine to give a guided tour of ecclesiol-
ogy—the theology of the church. I know of no better curriculum for generating understanding of and involvement in the church than this. It will be a welcome resource in
our church for years to come."

Rick Holland, Senior Pastor, Mission Road Bible Church, Prairie Village, Kansas

"In America today we have the largest churches in the history of our nation, but the
least amount of impact for Christ's kingdom. Slick marketing and finely polished vision
statements are a foundation of sand. The 9Marks Healthy Church Study Guides series
is a refreshing departure from church-growth materials, towards an in-depth study of
God's Word that will equip God's people with his vision for his Church. These study
guides will lead local congregations to abandon secular methodologies for church
growth and instead rely on Christ's principles for developing healthy, God-honoring
assemblies."

Carl J. Broggi, Senior Pastor, Community Bible Church, Beaufort, South Carolina;
President, Search the Scriptures Radio Ministry

"Anyone who loves Jesus will love what Jesus loves. The Bible clearly teaches that Jesus
loves the church. He knows about and cares for individual churches and wants them to
be spiritually healthy and vibrant. Not only has Jesus laid down his life for the church
but he has also given many instructions in his Word regarding how churches are to live
and function in the world. This series of Bible studies by 9Marks shows how Scripture
teaches these things. Any Christian who works through this curriculum, preferably
with other believers, will be helped to see in fresh ways the wisdom, love, and power of
God in establishing the church on earth. These studies are biblical, practical, and acces-
sible. I highly recommend this curriculum as a useful tool that will help any church
embrace its calling to display the glory of God to a watching world."

Thomas Ascol, Senior Pastor, Grace Baptist Church of Cape Coral, Florida;
Executive Director, Founders Ministries

9MARKS HEALTHY CHURCH STUDY GUIDES

GOD'S GOOD NEWS: THE GOSPEL

Bobby Jamieson
Mark Dever, General Editor
Jonathan Leeman, Managing Editor

HEALTHY CHURCH STUDY GUIDES

 **CROSSWAY**

WHEATON, ILLINOIS

Trade paperback ISBN: 978-1-4335-2536-0

PDF ISBN: 978-1-4335-2537-7

Mobipocket ISBN: 978-1-4335-2538-4

ePub ISBN: 978-1-4335-2539-1

Crossway is a publishing ministry of Good News Publishers.

LB		20	19	18	17	16	15	14	13	12
15	14	13	12	11	10	9	8	7	6	5	4	3	2	1

CONTENTS

INTRODUCTION

What does the local church mean to you?

Maybe you love your church. You love the people. You love the preaching and the singing. You can't wait to show up on Sunday, and you cherish fellowship with other church members throughout the week.

Then again, maybe your church is just a place you show up to a couple times a month. You sneak in late, duck out early.

We at 9Marks are convinced that the local church is where God means to display his glory to the nations. And we want to help you catch this vision, together with your whole church.

The 9Marks Healthy Church Study Guides are a series of six- or seven-week studies on each of the "nine marks of a healthy church" plus one introductory study. These nine marks are the core convictions of our ministry. To provide a quick introduction to them, we've included a chapter from Mark Dever's book *What Is a Healthy Church?* with each study. We don't claim that these nine marks are the most important things about the church or the only important things about the church. But we do believe that they are biblical and therefore helpful for churches.

So, in these studies, we're going to work through the biblical foundations and practical applications of each mark. The ten studies are:

- *Built upon the Rock: The Church* (the introductory study)
- *Hearing God's Word: Expositional Preaching*
- *The Whole Truth about God: Biblical Theology*
- *God's Good News: The Gospel*
- *Real Change: Conversion*
- *Reaching the Lost: Evangelism*
- *Committing to One Another: Church Membership*

- *Guarding One Another: Church Discipline*
- *Growing One Another: Discipleship in the Church*
- *Leading One Another: Church Leadership*

Each session of these studies takes a close look at one or more passages of Scripture and considers how to apply it to the life of your congregation. We hope they are equally appropriate for Sunday school, small groups, and other contexts where a group of two to two-hundred people can come together and discuss God's Word.

These studies are mainly driven by observation, interpretation, and application questions, so get ready to speak up! We also hope that these studies provide opportunities for people to reflect together on their experiences in the church, whatever those experiences may be.

What's the last piece of good news you heard? What made it so good? What difference did it make in your life?

As Christians, we are people of good news. We believe that the gospel of Jesus Christ is the best news in the world. And the gospel is just that: news. It's the announcement of what God has done in Christ to reconcile sinners to himself.

But how well do we know the gospel? Could you share the gospel with someone else off the top of your head?

The gospel is the most important message any of us have ever heard. So it's more than worth our while to spend a few weeks digging into its depth and riches. In this study we're going to explore the message of the gospel through the simple outline: God-Man-Christ-Response. And we're going to consider what it means to live a gospel-driven life, and to live together as a gospel-driven church. Let's find out what makes the good news so good!

AN ESSENTIAL MARK
OF A HEALTHY CHURCH:
A BIBLICAL UNDERSTANDING
OF THE GOOD NEWS

BY MARK DEVER

(Originally published as chapter 7 of What Is a Healthy Church?*)*

It is particularly important for our churches to have sound biblical theology in one special area—in our understanding of the good news of Jesus Christ, the gospel. The gospel is the heart of Christianity, and so it should be at the heart of our churches.

A healthy church is a church in which every member, young and old, mature and immature, unites around the wonderful good news of salvation through Jesus Christ. Every text in the Bible points to it or some aspect of it. So the church gathers week after week to hear the gospel rehearsed once again. A biblical understanding of the good news should inform every sermon, every act of baptism and communion, every song, every prayer, every conversation. More than anything else in the church's life, the members of a healthy church pray and long to know this gospel more deeply.

Why? Because the hope of the gospel is the hope of knowing the glory of God in the face of Christ (2 Cor. 4:6). It's the hope of seeing him clearly and knowing him fully, even as we are fully known (1 Cor. 13:12). It's the hope of becoming like him as we see him as he is (1 John 3:2).

GOSPEL BASICS

The gospel is not the news that we're okay. It's not the news that God is love. It's not the news that Jesus wants to be our friend. It's not the news that he has a wonderful plan or purpose for our life. The gospel is the good news that Jesus Christ died on the cross as a sacrificial substitute for sinners and rose again, making a way for us to be reconciled to God. It's the news that the Judge will become the Father, if only we repent and believe.

Here are four points I try to remember whenever sharing the gospel, whether in private or in public—(1) God, (2) man, (3) Christ, and (4) response. In other words:

- Have I explained that God is our holy and sovereign Creator?
- Have I made it clear that we humans are a strange mixture, wonderfully made in God's image yet horribly fallen, sinful, and separated from him?
- Have I explained who Jesus is and what he has done—that he is the God-man who uniquely and exclusively stands in between God and man as a substitute and resurrected Lord?
- And finally, even if I've shared all this, have I clearly stated that a person must respond to the gospel and must believe this message and so turn from his life of self-centeredness and sin?

Sometimes, it's tempting to present some of the very real benefits of the gospel as the gospel itself. And these benefits tend to be things that non-Christians naturally want, such as joy, peace, happiness, fulfillment, self-esteem, or love. Yet presenting them as the gospel is presenting a partial truth. And, as J. I. Packer says, "A half truth masquerading as the whole truth becomes a complete untruth."[1]

Fundamentally, we don't need just joy or peace or purpose. We need God himself. Since we are condemned sinners, then, we need his forgiveness above all else. We need spiritual life. When we present the gospel less radically, we simply ask for false conversions and increasingly meaningless church membership lists, both of which make the evangelization of the world around us more difficult.

[1]Quoted in J. I. Packer, "Saved by His Precious Blood: An Introduction to John Owen's *The Death of Death in the Death of Christ*" in J. I. Packer and Mark Dever, *In My Place Condemned He Stood: Celebrating the Glory of the Atonement* (Wheaton, IL: Crossway, 2008), 113.

GOSPEL OVERFLOW

When a church is healthy and its members know and cherish the gospel above everything else, they will increasingly want to share it with the world. George W. Truett, a great Christian leader of the past generation and pastor of First Baptist Church in Dallas, Texas, said:

> The supreme indictment that you can bring against a church . . . is that such a church lacks in passion and compassion for human souls. A church is nothing better than an ethical club if its sympathies for lost souls do not overflow, and if it does not go out to seek to point lost souls to the knowledge of Jesus Christ.

Today, the members of our churches will spend far more time with non-Christians in their homes, offices, and neighborhoods for far longer than they will spend with other Christians—let alone non-Christians—on Sundays. Evangelism is not something we mainly do by inviting someone to church. Each of us has tremendous news of salvation in Christ. Let's not barter it for something else. Let's share it today!

A healthy church knows the gospel, and a healthy church shares it.

WEEK 1
WHAT IS THE GOSPEL?

GETTING STARTED

What is the gospel of Jesus Christ? You'd think that would be an easy question for Christians to answer. But if you ask fifty professing evangelical Christians that question, you're likely to get almost as many answers!

1. What are some ways you've heard evangelical Christians define the gospel?

MAIN IDEA

The gospel is the good news about what God has done to save sinners through the sacrificial death and resurrection of Christ.

DIGGING IN

The most detailed, systematic discussion of the gospel in the whole Bible is found in Paul's letter to the Romans, especially in the first four chapters.

After announcing that he is not ashamed of the gospel because the righteousness of God is revealed in it (Rom. 1:16–17), Paul begins his proclamation of the good news by delivering some sobering *bad news* in 1:18 through 3:20:

> [18] For the wrath of God is revealed from heaven against all ungodliness and unrighteousness of men, who by their unrighteousness suppress the truth. (1:18)

> [21] For although they knew God, they did not honor him as God or give thanks to him, but they became futile in their thinking, and their foolish hearts were darkened. [22] Claiming to be wise, they became fools, [23] and exchanged the glory of the immortal God for images

resembling mortal man and birds and animals and creeping things. (1:21–23)

[1] Therefore you have no excuse, O man, every one of you who judges. For in passing judgment on another you condemn yourself, because you, the judge, practice the very same things. [2] We know that the judgment of God rightly falls on those who practice such things. (2:1–2)

[9] What then? Are we Jews any better off? No, not at all. For we have already charged that all, both Jews and Greeks, are under sin, [10] as it is written:

> "None is righteous, no, not one;
> [11] no one understands;
> no one seeks for God.
> [12] All have turned aside; together they have become worthless;
> no one does good,
> not even one." (3:9–12)

[19] Now we know that whatever the law says it speaks to those who are under the law, so that every mouth may be stopped, and the whole world may be held accountable to God. [20] For by works of the law no human being will be justified in his sight, since through the law comes knowledge of sin. (3:19–20)

1. To whom are human beings accountable? What passage(s) do you see this in?

2. What does God require of people? (Hint: See Rom. 1:21–23.)

3. Has any human being done what God requires of us? (Hint: See Rom. 3:9–12, 19–20.)

4. What are the results of humanity's universal rebellion against God? What is God's attitude toward humanity because of our sin? (Hint: See Rom. 1:18; 2:2; 3:19–20.)

5. Have you ever heard evangelistic presentations that minimized or ignored the bad news Paul explains in these chapters? If so,

- How would you evaluate them in light of these passages?
- What do you think the results of "gospel" messages that ignore sin and God's wrath will be?

6. What are some problems that people tend to present as our main problem when they share the gospel?

7. What, according to Paul, is the most fundamental problem people face?

To sum up, there are two main points that Paul is communicating in this three-chapter-long explanation of the bad news of humanity's rebellion against God:

1. All people are accountable to God, who is our holy Creator and Lord, and who is worthy of our worship and obedience.
2. All people have rebelled against God, continually sin against God, and are therefore objects of God's wrath.

Now, on to the *good news*:

[21] But now the righteousness of God has been manifested apart from the law, although the Law and the Prophets bear witness to it— [22] the righteousness of God through faith in Jesus Christ for all who believe. For there is no distinction: [23] for all have sinned and fall short of the glory of God, [24] and are justified by his grace as a gift, through the redemption that is in Christ Jesus, [25] whom God put forward as a propitiation by his blood, to be received by faith. This was to show God's righteousness, because in his divine forbearance he had passed over former sins. [26] It was to show his righteousness at the present time, so that he might be just and the justifier of the one who has faith in Jesus. (Rom. 3:21–26)

[4] Now to the one who works, his wages are not counted as a gift but as his due. [5] And to the one who does not work but believes in him who justifies the ungodly, his faith is counted as righteousness. (Rom. 4:4–5)

8. What is God's solution to the problem Paul has been expounding for three chapters?

9. According to Paul, how do people receive the salvation God offers in Christ?

10. The word "propitiation" (3:25) means "a sacrifice that satisfies and turns away God's wrath."

- a) Who needs to be propitiated? Why?
- b) Who does the propitiating? How?
- c) What is the result of Jesus's propitiating death *for God?* (Hint: See Rom. 3:26.)
- d) What is the result of Jesus's propitiating death *for those who believe in him?*

11. The word "justify" means "to declare someone to be righteous" (Rom. 3:24; 4:5; see also 3:20).

- According to Paul, on what basis can people be justified by God?
- Can we be justified by doing good works?

We could summarize Paul's explanation of the good news in these passages in two main points:

1. Through putting Christ forward as a propitiation, God has made a way for guilty sinners to have their sins wiped out, to have God's wrath turned away from them, and to be declared righteous in God's sight.
2. The way we receive this salvation is through faith in Jesus, by trusting him alone to save us, not any good works that we do.

Putting it all together, we could summarize the gospel in four words: God, Man, Christ, Response.

God. God is the creator of all things. He is perfectly holy, worthy of all worship, and will punish sin.

Man. All people, though created good, have become sinful by nature. From birth, all people are alienated from God, hostile to God, and subject to the wrath of God.

Christ. Jesus Christ, who is fully God and fully man, lived a sinless life, died on the cross to bear God's wrath in the place of all who would believe in him, and rose from the grave in order to give his people eternal life.

Response. God calls everyone everywhere to turn from their sins and trust in Christ in order to be saved.

12. Here are some common misunderstandings of the gospel. How would you respond to them in light of the passages we've just studied?

a) The gospel is that God wants us to live better lives.
b) The gospel is that God loves you and has a wonderful plan for your life.
c) The gospel is that God's kingdom has come in Jesus and now he calls us to work with him to transform every aspect of human society.
d) Can you think of others?

13. What do you think are some of the practical consequences of having a fuzzy definition of the gospel or a wrong definition of the gospel? What are some of the good results that should follow when we rightly define the gospel?

WEEK 2
GOD, THE RIGHTEOUS CREATOR

GETTING STARTED

1. *What do your non-Christian friends or family think about God? If they profess to believe in God, what do they believe* about *him?*

MAIN IDEA

A right understanding of the gospel begins with a right understanding of God: that he is the righteous Creator, and that we are all accountable to him.

DIGGING IN

In order to rightly understand the gospel, we need to begin where the whole Bible begins: with God the Creator. In Genesis 1 we read,

> [1] In the beginning, God created the heavens and the earth. [2] The earth was without form and void, and darkness was over the face of the deep. And the Spirit of God was hovering over the face of the waters. [3] And God said, "Let there be light," and there was light. (1:1–3)

In the rest of Genesis 1 we read of God creating the sea, the earth, plants, stars, and all kinds of animals. Then, as the culmination of God's creating work, we read,

> [26]Then God said, "Let us make man in our image, after our likeness. And let them have dominion over the fish of the sea and over the birds of the heavens and over the livestock and over all the earth and over every creeping thing that creeps on the earth."

^{27}So God created man in his own image,
in the image of God he created him;
male and female he created them. (1:26–27)

1. *What does Genesis 1 teach about the whole universe?*

2. *What does Genesis 1 teach about humankind?*

3. *Many people in the West today believe that matter is all that exists, that humans evolved through purely natural processes, and that there are, therefore, no absolute standards of morality. How does Genesis 1's account of creation confront these beliefs?*

4. *Many people in the West today think of themselves as subject to no one, and free to do whatever they want. How does Genesis 1 confront those attitudes?*

5. *Why is it important for people to understand that God is their Creator in order for them to understand that they need a savior?*

While Genesis 1 serves as a fountainhead of revelation about who God is as Creator, the rest of the Bible has plenty more to say about God's holy character. Consider God's revelation of his name to Moses in Exodus 34:

> ^{6} And he passed in front of Moses, proclaiming, "The LORD, the LORD, the compassionate and gracious God, slow to anger, abounding in love and faithfulness, maintaining love to thousands, and forgiving wickedness, rebellion and sin. ^{7} Yet he does not leave the guilty unpunished." (34:6–7 NIV)

6. *What are the aspects of God's character we see in this passage that people are generally happy to embrace? Why do you think people are generally happy to think about God in these ways?*

7. *What are the aspects of God's character we see in this passage that people generally reject or oppose? Why do you think people so often oppose these aspects of God's character?*

Countless other passages in Scripture testify that God is perfectly holy and righteous and that he will judge all people according to what they have done. Consider just a few:

> [5] This is the message we have heard from him and proclaim to you, that God is light, and in him is no darkness at all. (1 John. 1:5)

> [13] Your eyes are too pure to look on evil; you cannot tolerate wrongdoing. (Hab. 1:13 NIV)

> [5] But because of your hard and impenitent heart you are storing up wrath for yourself on the day of wrath when God's righteous judgment will be revealed.
> [6] He will render to each one according to his works: [7] to those who by patience in well-doing seek for glory and honor and immortality, he will give eternal life; [8] but for those who are self-seeking and do not obey the truth, but obey unrighteousness, there will be wrath and fury. (Rom. 2:5–8)

> [30] For we know him who said, "Vengeance is mine; I will repay." And again, "The Lord will judge his people." [31] It is a fearful thing to fall into the hands of the living God. (Heb. 10:30–31)

8. What do these passages teach about God's attitude toward sin? What do they say God will do to sin?

9. Many people in the West today think that morality is entirely determined by one's culture. How would you respond to someone who believed this in light of these passages?

10. Many people today view God as an indulgent, grandfatherly figure who makes no demands on us and is very understanding of the fact that we all make mistakes. How does that view hold up to what these passages teach us?

11. Why would you say it's important to tell our non-Christian friends that God is our righteous Creator when we attempt to share the gospel with them?

12. What are some ways that the church can testify that God is our righteous Creator:

    a) In corporate worship services?

    b) As members work throughout the week?

    c) In the church's expectations of its members?

WEEK 3
MAN, THE SINNER

GETTING STARTED
1. *When you share the gospel with others, are there any concepts that people seem just to not understand?*

2. *When you share the gospel with others, are there any concepts that people seem to get downright angry about?*

One core component of the gospel that people often either don't understand or angrily reject is the Bible's teaching about what humanity's basic problem is. So, we're going to devote our entire study to that topic.

MAIN IDEA
Humanity's fundamental problem is that we are all sinners by nature and by choice, and are therefore subject to the wrath of God.

DIGGING IN
Romans 3:9–20 is one of the clearest discussions of humanity's most basic problem in all of Scripture. In it, Paul writes,

> [9] What then? Are we Jews any better off? No, not at all. For we have already charged that all, both Jews and Greeks, are under sin, [10] as it is written:
>
> > "None is righteous, no, not one;
> > > [11] no one understands;
> > no one seeks for God.
> > [12] All have turned aside; together they have become worthless;
> > > no one does good,
> > > not even one."

[13] "Their throat is an open grave;
     they use their tongues to deceive."
"The venom of asps is under their lips."
[14] "Their mouth is full of curses and bitterness."
[15] "Their feet are swift to shed blood;
     [16] in their paths are ruin and misery,
     [17] and the way of peace they have not known."
[18] "There is no fear of God before their eyes."

[19] Now we know that whatever the law says it speaks to those who are under the law, so that every mouth may be stopped, and the whole world may be held accountable to God. [20] For by works of the law no human being will be justified in his sight, since through the law comes knowledge of sin. (3:9–20)

1. According to this passage, how many people are righteous in God's sight?

2. In verses 11 through 18, Paul gives several different examples from the Old Testament of the ways we sin. List as many as you can.

3. What does Paul's extensive catalogue of sins teach us about human nature?

4. In verse 11, Paul asserts that "no one seeks for God," and in verse 18 Paul finishes his catalogue of sins by saying, "There is no fear of God before their eyes." How do you think these sins relate to all the others Paul mentions?

5. Many people in our culture think that there is no standard of what's morally right and wrong for all people. They think that individual people or cultures simply decide what's right for them. In light of this passage, how would you respond to someone who believed that? (See especially v. 19.)

6. Read verse 19. What does it mean to be held accountable to God? Why will every mouth be stopped?

7. Read verse 20. In light of this verse, how would you respond to someone who said, "I'm generally a pretty good person. I'm sure that God will accept me in the end because I've done better than most people"?

As we saw in verse 19, the Bible teaches that sin is not just a problem for us simply because it has bad consequences in our own lives. Rather, consider what Paul says in Ephesians 5:

> [5] For you may be sure of this, that everyone who is sexually immoral or impure, or who is covetous (that is, an idolater), has no inheritance in the kingdom of Christ and God. [6] Let no one deceive you with empty words, for because of these things the wrath of God comes upon the sons of disobedience. (Eph. 5:5–6)

8. What does Paul say will happen to those who practice sexual immorality, impurity, or covetousness?

9. Upon whom does God's wrath come (v. 6)? Why?

10. In light of both of these passages, how would you describe humanity's natural condition before God?

11. As we've discussed in previous studies, the gospel is the good news about what God has done to save sinners through the death and resurrection of Jesus Christ. Why is it important to understand the Bible's teaching about our sin and God's wrath in order to understand and embrace the gospel?

12. Because we are all sinners before God, it is useless to compare ourselves with others in order to appear to be better than them before God. What does that say about our temptation to measure our spirituality by others?

13. What are some ways that the Bible's teaching on sin and God's wrath should impact the life of the church? Consider the following areas:

 a) Corporate Worship
 b) Preaching
 c) Discipleship relationships
 d) Evangelism

14. How should a biblical understanding of humanity's fundamental problem cause us to rejoice in the gospel?

WEEK 4
JESUS CHRIST, THE SAVIOR

GETTING STARTED
Our culture is filled with messages of self-salvation:

- "Deep down, all of us are beautiful, spiritual people. We just need to clean off the grime the world has rubbed onto us so that we can live by our pure, inner self."
- "If you work hard, save your money, and live right, you can have anything you want in life."

1. What are some other messages of self-salvation you've heard?

2. Have you ever encountered someone who thought Christianity was a message of self-salvation? What did they believe? How did you respond?

Far from being a religion of self-salvation, Christianity insists that we are totally unable to save ourselves from God's wrath. The Christian message, the gospel, is that through Jesus's death and resurrection, God has accomplished salvation, a salvation we could never achieve ourselves.

MAIN IDEA
In his death on the cross, Jesus Christ satisfied God's wrath against all those who would turn from their sin and trust in him. The heart of the gospel is the good news that Jesus has accomplished salvation for us through his death and resurrection.

DIGGING IN
In Isaiah 52:13–53:12, the prophet foresees a servant of the Lord who will suffer in order to save his people:

[13] Behold, my servant shall act wisely;
    he shall be high and lifted up,
    and shall be exalted.
[14] As many were astonished at you—
    his appearance was so marred, beyond human semblance,
    and his form beyond that of the children of mankind—
[15] so shall he sprinkle many nations;
    kings shall shut their mouths because of him;
for that which has not been told them they see,
    and that which they have not heard they understand.

[53:1] Who has believed what he has heard from us?
    And to whom has the arm of the LORD been revealed?
[2] For he grew up before him like a young plant,
    and like a root out of dry ground;
he had no form or majesty that we should look at him,
    and no beauty that we should desire him.
[3] He was despised and rejected by men;
    a man of sorrows, and acquainted with grief;
and as one from whom men hide their faces
    he was despised, and we esteemed him not.

[4] Surely he has borne our griefs
    and carried our sorrows;
yet we esteemed him stricken,
    smitten by God, and afflicted.
[5] But he was pierced for our transgressions;
    he was crushed for our iniquities;
upon him was the chastisement that brought us peace,
    and with his wounds we are healed.
[6] All we like sheep have gone astray;
    we have turned—every one—to his own way;
and the LORD has laid on him
    the iniquity of us all.

[7] He was oppressed, and he was afflicted,
    yet he opened not his mouth;
like a lamb that is led to the slaughter,
    and like a sheep that before its shearers is silent,
    so he opened not his mouth.
[8] By oppression and judgment he was taken away;

and as for his generation, who considered
that he was cut off out of the land of the living,
   stricken for the transgression of my people?
[9] And they made his grave with the wicked
   and with a rich man in his death,
although he had done no violence,
   and there was no deceit in his mouth.

[10] Yet it was the will of the LORD to crush him;
   he has put him to grief;
when his soul makes an offering for guilt,
   he shall see his offspring; he shall prolong his days;
the will of the LORD shall prosper in his hand.
[11] Out of the anguish of his soul he shall see and be satisfied;
by his knowledge shall the righteous one, my servant,
   make many to be accounted righteous,
   and he shall bear their iniquities.
[12] Therefore I will divide him a portion with the many,
   and he shall divide the spoil with the strong,
because he poured out his soul to death
   and was numbered with the transgressors;
yet he bore the sin of many,
   and makes intercession for the transgressors.

In Acts 8, we read that an Ethiopian eunuch was reading this passage, and Philip, "beginning with this Scripture," told him to good news about Jesus (Acts 8:31–35). Jesus himself cited this passage and said, "For I tell you that this Scripture must be fulfilled in me" (Luke 22:37). So we know from Scripture itself that this passage was fulfilled in Jesus Christ.

1. The figure in this passage is often referred to as the "suffering servant." Going through the whole passage in order, list all the different ways this servant suffers.

2. Who causes the servant to suffer? (Hint: There's more than one answer.)

3. What is the reason for the servant's suffering? Is it something he did?

GOD'S GOOD NEWS

4. *Substitution—the fact that the servant stands in the place of his people—is one of this passage's most prominent themes. List all the places where this passage speaks of the servant suffering or otherwise acting in the place of his people. Put what the servant does in the "He/His" column and what is spoken of as "ours" in the "We/Our" column:*

He/His	We/Our	(Verse)
		(53:4)
		(53:4)
		(53:5)
		(53:5)
		(53:5)
		(53:5)
		(53:6)
		(53:8)
		(53:10)
		(53:11)
		(53:11)
		(53:12)

5. *Looking at the passage as a whole, how would you summarize in your own words:*

- What the servant suffered on behalf of his people?
- What the result of his suffering is *for* his people?

Because it points forward so clearly to Jesus's crucifixion, this passage proclaims the heart of the gospel to us. We can summarize this passage's teaching about Jesus's death in the words "penal substitutionary atonement."

- **Penal:** Jesus's death paid the *penalty* for the sins of his people. God punished him as if he were guilty of their sins.
- **Substitutionary:** On the cross, Jesus stood in the place of his people. He was a *substitute*. He suffered so that they wouldn't. He was punished so that they would be healed and reconciled to God. He was counted guilty so that they would be counted righteous.

- **Atonement:** Jesus poured out his life as an offering for sin. He *atoned* for our sin, covering it over and making us *at one* with God. Where there was enmity, now there is peace. In his substitutionary death, Jesus fully satisfied the demands of God's justice so that all who turn to him in faith are counted righteous in God's sight, accepted by God, reconciled to God, and given eternal life.

This is the heart of the gospel: Jesus suffered God's wrath on the cross so that all who trust in him will be justified—counted righteous by God!—by faith alone.

6. *This passage clearly states that the servant suffers unto death—that he gives his life as a substitutionary sacrifice (Isa. 53:8–10, 12). Yet the passage also speaks of the servant seeing his offspring, prolonging his days, and receiving a reward from the Lord because he poured out his soul to death (Isa. 53:10–12). How can both of these things be?*

7. *As we've just seen, this passage clearly points forward not only to Jesus's substitutionary death but also to his resurrection.*

- Would the gospel be good news if Jesus never rose from the grave? What do you think? (See Isa. 53:12.)
- How would the apostle Paul answer this question? (Hint: See 1 Cor. 15:17–19.)

8. *Have you ever heard an evangelistic presentation which did not explain Jesus's crucifixion and resurrection? Was that actually a presentation of the gospel?*

9. *Believing the good news about Jesus's death and resurrection is not only how we become Christians—it fuels our growth as Christians, too. How does the gospel address:*

- a) Wrongly craving others' approval and acceptance?
- b) Cultural or ethnic prejudice?
- c) Anxiety about the future?
- d) Greed?
- e) Can you name issues you struggle with, and how the gospel addresses them?

10. Why is it important for a church to constantly rehearse, celebrate, and center its life around the good news about Jesus's death and resurrection?

11. What are some ways that a local church can rehearse, celebrate, and center its life around Jesus's saving work on the cross?

    a) In its times of corporate worship?
- In the sermons?
- In the songs it sings?
- In corporate prayer?

    b) In small groups?

    c) In community outreach efforts?

    d) In . . . can you think of other areas of the church's life?

FOR FURTHER STUDY

If you'd like to think more about the atonement, consider reading:

J. I. Packer and Mark Dever, *In My Place Condemned He Stood* (Crossway, 2008)

Leon Morris, *The Atonement* (InterVarsity, 1984)

Mark Dever and Michael Lawrence, *It Is Well: Expositions on Substitutionary Atonement* (Crossway, 2010)

WEEK 5
OUR RESPONSE:
REPENTANCE AND FAITH

GETTING STARTED

When people in our culture talk about "faith," they might mean "hoping something is true even though all the evidence in the world is against it." Or they might mean bare intellectual assent that has no impact on someone's life: "I believe in God, but that doesn't mean I'm a religious nut or something." Some people think that faith is simply an optimistic confidence that life is going to turn out all right: "Just have faith. Things will get better."

1. Have you heard people use the word "faith" in these ways? What do you think the average person today understands "faith" to be?

2. Do you think a person can believe in Jesus without that faith changing his or her life?

MAIN IDEA

The gospel calls all people to repent of their sin and believe in Jesus Christ in order to be saved.

DIGGING IN

As we've discussed in the past few studies, the gospel is the good news about what God has done to save sinners through the death and resurrection of Christ. But, unlike much of the news you may read or hear every day, this news demands a response.

Throughout the New Testament, we see that the proper response to the gospel has two components, like two sides of a coin. Consider the following passages:

- In Mark 1:15 Jesus says, "The time is fulfilled, and the kingdom of God is at hand; repent and believe in the gospel."
- In Acts 20:21 Paul explained his ministry by saying, "I have declared to both Jews and Greeks that they must turn to God in repentance and have faith in our Lord Jesus" (NIV).

1. What are the two elements of the right response to the gospel we see in these passages?

Repentance and faith always go together. But in order to understand each of them clearly, we're going to consider them in turn: first repentance, then faith.

There are many texts in the New Testament that command people to repent or describe what it means to repent:

- In Acts 3:19–20, after proclaiming the message about Jesus's death, Peter says, "Repent therefore, and turn back, that your sins may be blotted out, that times of refreshing may come from the presence of the Lord, and that he may send the Christ appointed for you, Jesus."
- In Acts 26:20, Paul says that he declares to both Jews and Gentiles "that they should repent and turn to God, performing deeds in keeping with their repentance."
- In 1 Thessalonians 1:9–10, Paul reminds the Thessalonians of their conversion: "For they themselves report concerning us the kind of reception we had among you, and how you turned to God from idols to serve the living and true God, and to wait for his Son from heaven, whom he raised from the dead, Jesus who delivers us from the wrath to come."

2. What other term is used in all three of these passages to describe repentance?

3. What do these passages say people are to turn from*? What, or who, are we to turn to? List specific examples.*

4. According to these passages, repentance is not merely a one-time event. Rather, it has radical, ongoing implications in the life of a believer. What implications of repentance do these passages show us?

5. In light of the passages we've studied, how would you respond to someone who claimed to believe in Jesus but said that they don't think they need to repent of their sins and submit to Jesus as Lord?

The other side of the coin is faith. In Romans 4, Paul paints a picture of genuine faith, drawn from the life of Abraham. He writes,

[18] In hope he believed against hope, that he should become the father of many nations, as he had been told, "So shall your offspring be." [19] He did not weaken in faith when he considered his own body, which was as good as dead (since he was about a hundred years old), or when he considered the barrenness of Sarah's womb. [20] No unbelief made him waver concerning the promise of God, but he grew strong in his faith as he gave glory to God, [21] fully convinced that God was able to do what he had promised. [22] That is why his faith was "counted to him as righteousness." [23] But the words "it was counted to him" were not written for his sake alone, [24] but for ours also. It will be counted to us who believe in him who raised from the dead Jesus our Lord, [25] who was delivered up for our trespasses and raised for our justification. (4:18–25)

6. What had God promised to do for Abraham? (For background, see Genesis 15:1–6.)

7. What reasons did Abraham have to doubt God's promise (v. 19)?

8. What was Abraham's attitude toward God's promise (vv. 20–21)? What does this teach us about faith?

Some people today think of faith as simply belief in facts, mere mental assent. They think that someone can believe in Jesus the way we might believe that Abraham Lincoln was born in a log cabin in Kentucky. That may well be a true belief, but it doesn't require anything more than mental assent on my part, and it certainly doesn't affect my life in any meaningful way.

But when the Bible talks about faith, it means wholehearted trust. Faith is like jumping off a diving board because you know that there's eight feet of water between you and the concrete bottom of the pool. You trust the water, so to speak, so you fling yourself into the air above it.

True faith, therefore, always produces a changed life. If you trust in Christ, you'll believe, and *do*, what he says. There's no way to believe in Jesus but say, "I don't think you get to tell me what to do with my life." Jesus Christ is Lord. He is the King of the universe. To believe in him is to accept that claim. It's to rely on him for salvation, which involves turning your whole self away from sin and to Christ.

9. What did God do in response to Abraham's faith (v. 22)? What does this have to do with us (vv. 23–25)?

In this passage Paul proclaims the glorious truth that we are justified by faith alone. That is, when we believe in Jesus Christ, God counts Jesus's perfect righteousness to us. Our past, present, and future sins are completely forgiven and our salvation is secure. All this happens solely on the basis of what Jesus has done for us.

10. The gospel message calls us to have faith in Jesus—that is, to trust in him and rely totally on him for salvation. What other things are you tempted to rely on to make you right with God?

11. How should a biblical understanding of our response to the gospel—turning from sin and trusting in Christ—impact:

　　a) How you interact with non-Christians?
　　b) Whom the church accepts as members?
　　c) Your relationships in the church?

WEEK 6
THE GOSPEL-DRIVEN LIFE

GETTING STARTED

1. *What are some things that encourage you the most as you seek to grow as a Christian?*

2. *What are some things that discourage you the most as you seek to grow as a Christian?*

MAIN IDEA

The gospel is not only the means by which we become Christians; it is also what enables us to grow as Christians.

DIGGING IN

In the first five chapters of Romans, Paul proclaims the free salvation which God grants in the gospel to all who believe in Christ. In chapter 6, Paul anticipates and answers a question that sinful people will naturally ask when we hear about the free grace of God:

> [1] What shall we say then? Are we to continue in sin that grace may abound? [2] By no means! How can we who died to sin still live in it? [3] Do you not know that all of us who have been baptized into Christ Jesus were baptized into his death? [4] We were buried therefore with him by baptism into death, in order that, just as Christ was raised from the dead by the glory of the Father, we too might walk in newness of life.
>
> [5] For if we have been united with him in a death like his, we shall certainly be united with him in a resurrection like his. [6] We know that our old self was crucified with him in order that the body of sin might be brought to nothing, so that we would no longer be enslaved to sin. [7] For one who has died has been set free from sin. [8] Now if we have died with Christ, we believe that we will also live with him. [9] We

know that Christ, being raised from the dead, will never die again; death no longer has dominion over him. ¹⁰ For the death he died he died to sin, once for all, but the life he lives he lives to God. ¹¹ So you also must consider yourselves dead to sin and alive to God in Christ Jesus.

¹² Let not sin therefore reign in your mortal body, to make you obey its passions. ¹³ Do not present your members to sin as instruments for unrighteousness, but present yourselves to God as those who have been brought from death to life, and your members to God as instruments for righteousness. ¹⁴ For sin will have no dominion over you, since you are not under law but under grace. (Rom. 6:1–14)

1. What question does Paul address in this passage?

2. Why do you think he addresses this particular question?

3. List all the different things Paul says have already happened to us who believe in Christ:

4. By what means have all these things happened to us? (Hint: See especially verse 5.)

As we learn in this passage, through faith in Christ we not only have our sins forgiven but we're given an entirely new nature. When we put our faith in Christ, our old self died—in fact, our old self was crucified—and we were raised to a new spiritual life through union with Christ.

The gospel not only gives us a new status before God, it gives us a new *self*—a self that is no longer enslaved to sin but is able to obey God by the power of the Spirit.

5. In this passage Paul commands us to do a number of things. List all of them below:

6. In verse 11 Paul gives the first command in the entire book of Romans: "So you also must consider yourselves dead to sin and alive to God in Christ Jesus."

   a) Explain this instruction in your own words.

b) Why do you think Paul tells us to basically think about ourselves differently before he gives any other specific commands?

7. Read verses 13 and 14. What reason or ground does Paul give in verse 14 for his instruction in verse 13?

8. What is this reason Paul gives such an encouragement to persevere in overcoming sin and pursuing righteousness?

9. If you trust in Christ for salvation, then according to this passage you've been united to Christ in his death and resurrection, which means:

- You've died to sin (v. 2).
- Your old self was crucified with Christ (v. 6).
- You've been set free from sin (v. 7).
- You've been brought from death to life (v. 13).

What are some specific sins you struggle with? How does this passage's teaching equip you to overcome those sins?

10. Many Christians think that the gospel is simply how we become Christians and then it's up to us to grow in holiness. What does this passage teach us about how the gospel relates to our growth as Christians?

11. As Justin Taylor has put it, most evangelical preaching on how to grow as a Christian goes something like this:

You are not _____;

You should be _____;

Therefore, do or be _____![1]

How does Paul's teaching in this passage differ from this common way of teaching Christians how to grow?

---

[1]Justin Taylor, "Imperatives-Indicatives=Impossibilities," *Between Two Worlds*, May 3, 2010, http://thegospelcoalition.org/blogs/justintaylor/2010/05/03/imperatives-indicatives-impossibilities/.

12. How would you apply Paul's teaching in this passage to someone who struggled with:

    a) Bitterness and envy toward others?

    b) Discouragement?

    c) An addiction?

WEEK 7
THE GOSPEL-DRIVEN
CHURCH

GETTING STARTED

1. Is there anything in your life that you have to do but you're unmotivated to do, or struggle to find the motivation to do?

2. Where do you think you could find the motivation to do these things?

In this study we're going to discover how the gospel motivates and equips us to build each other up in the church.

MAIN IDEA

The gospel not only frees us from sin individually, it also equips us to live together as a church in a way that builds unity, helps others grow spiritually, and brings glory to God.

DIGGING IN

After eleven chapters of expounding the gospel of God's grace, in Romans 12 Paul turns to exhort us about how to live in light of the gospel. In Romans 12:1–2 he writes,

> ¹ I appeal to you therefore, brothers, by the mercies of God, to present your bodies as a living sacrifice, holy and acceptable to God, which is your spiritual worship. ² Do not be conformed to this world, but be transformed by the renewal of your mind, that by testing you may discern what is the will of God, what is good and acceptable and perfect.

1. On what basis does Paul appeal to us in this passage?

2. What is Paul referring to when he speaks of "the mercies of God"?

3. In verse 2, what does Paul tell us not *to do? What does he tell us to do? How are we to do this?*

Immediately after this opening exhortation, Paul fleshes out what he means in very practical terms:

> ³ For by the grace given to me I say to everyone among you not to think of himself more highly than he ought to think, but to think with sober judgment, each according to the measure of faith that God has assigned. ⁴ For as in one body we have many members, and the members do not all have the same function, ⁵ so we, though many, are one body in Christ, and individually members one of another. ⁶ Having gifts that differ according to the grace given to us, let us use them: if prophecy, in proportion to our faith; ⁷ if service, in our serving; the one who teaches, in his teaching; ⁸ the one who exhorts, in his exhortation; the one who contributes, in generosity; the one who leads, with zeal; the one who does acts of mercy, with cheerfulness.
> ⁹ Let love be genuine. Abhor what is evil; hold fast to what is good. ¹⁰ Love one another with brotherly affection. Outdo one another in showing honor. ¹¹ Do not be slothful in zeal, be fervent in spirit, serve the Lord. ¹² Rejoice in hope, be patient in tribulation, be constant in prayer. ¹³ Contribute to the needs of the saints and seek to show hospitality. (Rom. 12:3–13)

4. List all the things Paul exhorts us to do in this passage in the chart below, along with the verse each one is found in. As you do, indicate whether this is a command that is primarily individual or corporate. That is, is it something you simply do yourself, or does it involve relating to others in the church?

Command (v. ___)	Individual or Corporate?

In verse 3, Paul gives his first example of what it means not to be conformed to this world but to be transformed by the renewal of our minds: "For by the grace given to me I say to everyone among you not to think of himself more highly than he ought to think, but to think with sober judgment, each according to the measure of faith that God has assigned."

5. How does the gospel equip us to think of ourselves with sober judgment?

6. What will be some of the results in our relationships if we think of ourselves more highly than we ought to?

7. What will be some of the results in our relationships if we think of ourselves with sober judgment?

8. Here's another implication of the gospel that Paul addresses: since we are in Christ by faith, we are all members of the same body. What does Paul exhort us to do in light of this? (See vv. 4–8)

9. What are some ways that you can seek to build up others through gifts God has given you?

10. How does the gospel equip and motivate us to genuinely love others with brotherly affection and to outdo each other in showing honor (vv. 9–10)?

11. In verse 13 Paul urges us, "Contribute to the needs of the saints and seek to show hospitality." How does the gospel empower and motivate us to care for others' needs in the church and to extend hospitality?

12. What are some practical ways that you can contribute to the needs of the saints and show hospitality?

13. *Widows are one group in the church who have particular needs, and whom God has a special concern for (Ps. 68:5). What are some practical ways you and others in your church can work to care for these dear saints?*

14. *In Romans 15:7, at the very end of his extended discussion of how we should live as a church in light of the gospel, Paul sums everything up by saying, "Therefore welcome one another as Christ has welcomed you, for the glory of God." What are some other practical ways you can think of that we can welcome each other in the church instead of creating division and disunity?*

TEACHER'S NOTES FOR WEEK 1

DIGGING IN

1. Human beings are accountable to God, our Creator and Ruler. Romans 3:19 says that the law condemns our sin so that the whole world may be accountable to God. Romans 1:18 says that God's wrath is revealed against us, which indicates our moral accountability to him. Romans 2:2 says that God's judgment falls on those who practice evil, which again indicates our ultimate accountability to God.

2. God requires that people give him the honor, thanks, and worship that he is due.

3. In Romans 2:1–2; 3:9–12; and 3:19–20 Paul argues that all people without exception have rebelled against God, sinned against him, and failed to do what he requires of us.

4. The results of humanity's rebellion against God include:

- Our thinking has become futile (1:21).
- Our hearts have become darkened (1:21).
- We've claimed to be wise but have become fools (1:22).
- We've degraded ourselves by worshiping idols (1:23).

And, most fundamentally, because of our sin, God's attitude toward us is wrath. God is angry with us because of our sin and will punish us for our sin, unless we repent of sin and trust in Christ.

5. Answers will vary.

6. Many professing Christians' evangelism communicates that our main problem is:

- Disease, death, or poverty
- Broken relationships
- Low self-esteem
- Lack of purpose in life
- Political oppression

7. According to Paul, the most fundamental problem people face is the wrath of God. *God* is our problem because we have all sinned against him, he is perfectly holy and righteous, and he will punish all sin.

8. God's solution to the problem Paul has expounded is the sacrificial death and resurrection of Christ.

9. People receive this salvation by faith, by trusting in Christ alone to save (vv. 23, 25). True faith involves recognizing that one is a sinner and turning from that sin, which the Bible calls "repentance."

10. Regarding the propitiation, the wrath-satisfying sacrifice of Jesus which verse 25 discusses:

    a) God is the one who needs to be propitiated, because his wrath is rightly against us because of our sin.

    b) Jesus (sent and commissioned by God the Father, and in obedience to God the Father) is the one who does the propitiating, by bearing the punishment we deserved for our sin on the cross.

    c) The result of Jesus's propitiating death *for God* is that he is now "just and the justifier of the one who has faith in Jesus" (v. 26). That is, God is both righteous, because he has punished sin exactly as it deserves, and he is able to *declare to be righteous* those who trust in Jesus, even though they are sinners.

    d) The result of Jesus's propitiating death *for those who believe in him* is that we are justified through faith in him alone. That is, when we trust in Jesus, God counts Jesus's righteousness to us, meaning that we are perfectly righteous in God's sight and all our sins are forgiven.

11. According to Paul, people can be justified on the basis of Christ's sacrifice, which atones for their sins (3:24–26), and his righteousness, which God counts to them (4:4–5). We receive this atoning sacrifice and righteousness through faith in Christ (3:22, 25, 26; 4:5).

12–13. There is a range of valid answers.

TEACHER'S NOTES FOR WEEK 2

DIGGING IN

1. Genesis 1 teaches that the whole universe was created by God and that he is therefore its Lord and Ruler.

2. Genesis 1 teaches that God created man in his image and gave him dominion over the earth. One implication of this is that man has a special relationship to God, in which he is supposed to represent God to the creation. Another implication is that all people are accountable to God our Creator for how we live.

3. Genesis 1 confronts these evolutionary beliefs by asserting that God created the universe out of nothing and that he created humanity by a special, direct act. This means that the moral conclusion some draw from belief in evolution—that there is no absolute standard of morality external to humanity—is wrong. Instead, Genesis 1 lays the foundation for understanding that morality is determined by conformity to the character and will of God.

4. Genesis 1's teaching that God is the Creator and therefore the Owner, Ruler, and Lord of all confronts these autonomous attitudes by teaching that all people are fundamentally creatures. We're derivative beings. We get our life from another, which means that we are at his disposal and must conform our lives to his will. In other words, the fact that God created us means that we are accountable to him in all we do.

5. In order for people to know that they need a savior, it's important for them to understand that God is their Creator because they need to understand that they are accountable to him. When we understand that God is our Creator, we realize that we can't simply live however we want. Rather, we are accountable to God for our every thought, word, and deed.

6. People are generally happy to embrace God's compassion, grace, patience, love, and forgiveness. One obvious reason for this is that, at least on the surface, all of these aspects of God's character seem to indicate that he has a favorable attitude *toward us*!

7. People tend to oppose God's righteousness and justice, those aspects of his character that guarantee that he *will* punish sin, as verse 7 describes. One reason people so often oppose these aspects of God's character is that

if God is holy, we can't simply live however we want and get away with it. If God is righteous, then he makes moral demands on our lives that we may not want to live with.

8. These passages teach us that God is totally free from sin, is completely opposed to sin, and will punish sin and sinners.

9. In light of these passages, one could respond to someone who held such relativist beliefs by explaining that the Bible teaches that morality is grounded in God's character. This means that it is universal and consistent, not relative to different cultures. Moreover, passages like these teach that God not only requires people to live a certain way, but that people will be finally, eternally held accountable by God for how they have lived.

10. These passages explode the "benign grandfather" view of God by demonstrating that God is holy, righteous, and utterly, morally pure. These passages also teach that, far from sweeping sin under the rug like an unscrupulous janitor (to borrow a phrase from Greg Gilbert's book *What Is the Gospel?*[2]), God is so intensely holy, righteous, and *good* that he will punish evil and all those who do evil.

11. There is a range of possible answers, but the basic idea is that in order to know why they need a savior, people need to understand:

- that God exists
- that God is the Creator and Lord of all
- that God is perfectly righteous and holy—that he is utterly morally perfect
- that we are all accountable to God for our actions
- that God will punish all sin

12. There is a range of valid answers. Here's a sample of ways the church can testify that God is our righteous Creator.

    a) In the church's corporate worship services:
- Acknowledging our dependence on him through prayers of petition
- Confessing in prayer how we've sinned against God and need his forgiveness
- Singing songs that magnify God for his power displayed in creation and for his holy character

---

[2]Greg Gilbert, *What Is the Gospel?* (Wheaton, IL: Crossway, 2010), 43.

b) As members work throughout the week:
   - Trust that the God who made us will provide for us, which will lead to radically generous use of money and other resources
   - Treat all people—regardless of age, gender, social status, ethnicity, or anything else—with compassion, respect, and love, since all people are made in God's image

c) In the church's expectations of its members:
   - In view of God's holy character, churches should expect that their members will pursue lives of holiness, continually repenting of sin and striving to image God's character to those around them

TEACHER'S NOTES FOR WEEK 3

DIGGING IN

1. According to this passage, no one is righteous in God's sight, not even one (vv. 11–12).

2. Examples of the ways we sin include:

- Deceiving others (v. 13)
- Cursing others, speaking bitterly (v. 14)
- Acting violently (v. 15)
- Causing others ruin and misery (v. 16)
- Not fearing God (v. 18)

3. Paul's catalogue of sins teaches us that humans are thoroughly corrupt, that sin permeates every facet of our being.

4. By opening his catalog of sins with "no one seeks for God" and finishing by saying, "There is no fear of God before their eyes," Paul seems to be indicating that the root cause of all of these different sins is that people have rejected God, rebelled against him, and refuse to fear and honor him as we ought.

5. An appropriate response to such a moral relativist would be something like, "According to Scripture, what's morally right and wrong is determined by God's own character, which doesn't change. Therefore, God holds all of us accountable to live in a way that is consistent with his character and will, whatever cultural tradition we live in."

6. To be held accountable by God means giving an account to God for all that we have done, receiving God's verdict on us for our actions, and receiving from God what our actions deserve, which, apart from faith in Christ, will be eternal punishment. Every mouth will be stopped because no one will be able to dispute God's verdict of "guilty."

7. In light of verse 19, an appropriate response would be something like, "God does not grade on a curve. The Bible teaches that no one can be justified, that is, declared righteous by God, on the basis of good works that we do. That's because none of us obey God 100 percent of the time, and God

rightly demands perfect obedience from us. Moreover, Scripture teaches not only that we're not perfect, but that all of us are sinful by nature."

8. Paul says that those who practice such things have no inheritance in the kingdom of Christ and God, which means that they will be excluded from God's kingdom on the last day and punished for their sin.

9. God's wrath comes upon the "sons of disobedience," which means all whose lives are characterized by sin. Why? Because God is perfectly righteous and holy and opposes all sin.

10. *The basic idea is that:*

- All people are sinners
- God's wrath is against us because of our sin

11. Answers will vary, but the basic idea is that we need to know what kind of a problem we're in, and that we have a problem at all, before we will embrace a savior.

12. Because God's holiness is our standard, and because God gifts and empowers us all individually by the Holy Spirit with gifts that differ according to God's will, we should *not* fundamentally evaluate ourselves by comparing ourselves with others. Rather, we should be humbled by the exacting standard of God's holiness *and* encouraged by the work of God's grace in our lives.

13. Answers will vary.

14. Answers will vary. The basic idea is that when we understand the depth of our problem, we will personally feel and rejoice in the glory of the solution. When we understand that we were enslaved to sin, we rejoice all the more that Christ has freed us from that slavery. When we understand that God's wrath was against us because of our sin, we rejoice that Christ has paid that penalty, and we are now reconciled to God and righteous in his sight. And so on.

TEACHER'S NOTES FOR WEEK 4

DIGGING IN

1. Here are all the ways the servant suffers in this passage:

- His appearance was marred, which speaks to physical suffering (52:14).
- He was despised and rejected by men (53:3).
- He was a man of sorrows, acquainted with grief (53:3).
- Men despised him, and his own people did not esteem him (53:3).
- He bore our griefs (53:4).
- He carried our sorrows (53:4).
- He appeared to us stricken by God, smitten, and afflicted (53:4).
- He was wounded for our transgressions (53:5).
- He was crushed for our iniquities (53:5).
- He was chastised for our peace (53:5).
- He was beaten for our healing (53:5).
- God laid our iniquity on him (53:6).
- He was oppressed and afflicted (53:7).
- He was taken away by oppression and judgment (53:8).
- He was cut off from the land of the living (i.e., killed; 53:8).
- He was stricken for the people's transgression (53:8).
- God crushed him and put him to grief (53:10).
- His soul makes an offering for sin (53:10).
- His soul is in anguish (53:11).
- He poured out his soul to death (53:12).

2. Men cause the servant to suffer (53:3, 7–9). But it's not only men: verse 10 tells us that it was the will of the Lord to crush him, and that he, *God*, has put him to grief. Verse 6 says, "And the LORD has laid on him the iniquity of us all." This means that God is the one, ultimately, who is punishing the servant and causing him to suffer.

3. The cause of the servant's suffering is God's punishment for his people's sin (53:4–6, etc.). The servant does *not* suffer for anything he does.

4. Here's what the completed chart should look like:

He/His	We/Our	(Verse)
Has borne	Our griefs	(53:4)
Carried	Our sorrows	(53:4)
Was pierced	For our transgressions	(53:5)
Was crushed	For our iniquities	(53:5)
Chastisement	Brought us peace	(53:5)
Wounds	Healed	(53:5)
The Lord laid on him	Our iniquity	(53:6)
Was stricken	For our transgressions	(53:8)
Makes an offering	For guilt (implicitly, ours)	(53:10)
Knowledge	Accounted righteous	(53:11)
Bear	His people's iniquities	(53:11)
Bore	The sin of many	(53:12)

5. The servant suffered God's wrath against God's people's sins (53:5–6). His physical suffering was the outward expression of his bearing God's wrath for the sins of many (53:10, 12), and this substitutionary sin-bearing cost him his life (53:8, 10, 12). The result for God's people is that they are "accounted righteous" in God's sight (53:11), are healed (53:5), and are given peace with God (53:5). In other words, through the servant's suffering, God's people are forgiven, reconciled to God, restored to a right relationship with God, and healed from the effects of sin.

6. How can the servant give his life as an offering for sin *and* see his off-spring, prolong his days, and receive a portion from the Lord? The answer is found in Jesus's resurrection from the dead. Jesus gave his life as an offering for sin and rose on the third day, proving that he had in fact satisfied God's wrath and becoming the source of eternal life for all who would believe in him.

7. No, the gospel would not be good news if Christ never rose from the grave, because his death would ultimately have been no different than any other crucifixion. It is Christ's resurrection that demonstrates and guar-antees the power of what his death on the cross accomplished. And the apostle Paul, of course, argues that if Christ was not raised from the dead,

our faith is futile, we're still in our sins, and we are to be pitied above all men (1 Cor. 15:17–19).

8. If an "evangelistic presentation" doesn't explain the meaning of Jesus's death and resurrection, then the gospel has not been presented.

9–11. Answers will vary.

TEACHER'S NOTES FOR WEEK 5

DIGGING IN

1. The two elements of a right response to the gospel are repentance and faith.

2. All three of these passages use the word "turn" to describe repentance, as in, to turn *from* sin and turn *to* God.

3. These passages say that we are to turn from sin and idols *to* God, to serve and obey him. See especially 1 Thessalonians 1:9.

4. First, we are to perform deeds in keeping with repentance. This means continually renouncing sin and seeking to obey God (Acts 26:20). Second, we now serve God instead of idols, which means that our whole lives are to be devoted to doing God's will (1 Thess. 1:9). Third, we have a new hope in Christ. So, repentance also means that we have determined to no longer set our hope on fleeting, earthly joys, but on Christ, whose coming we eagerly await (1 Thess. 1:10; see also Acts 3:20).

5. An appropriate response would be something like, "True faith can never be separated from repentance. To truly believe in Christ as Savior means that you recognize yourself to be a sinner, you recognize that your sin is abhorrent to God, and you depend on Christ to save you from sin. You can't genuinely do that without at the same time renouncing sin and resolving to no longer live in it."

6. God had promised that Abraham's offspring would be as numerous as the stars (Gen 15:5).

7. *Abraham's reasons to doubt God's promise were:*

- He was almost a hundred years old
- His wife Sarah was barren and also well advanced in years! (See Rom. 4:19)

8. Abraham's faith in God's promise didn't waver, but he was fully convinced that God was able to do what he had promised (Rom. 4:20–21). This teaches us that faith relies on God's power to fulfill his promises, even when they look impossible from a human perspective.

9. In response to Abraham's faith, God counted righteousness to him—that is, he declared him to be righteous, even though Abraham himself was a sinner. What does this have to do with us? Everything! Just as Abraham was justified by faith in Christ, we also are justified by faith and have Christ's righteousness counted to us (vv. 22–25).

10. Answers will vary.

11. Answers will vary. Regarding church membership, in light of the Bible's teaching on faith and repentance, it is important for the church to accept as members only people who have repented of their sin and trust in Christ, and whose lives show some fruit of those realities.

TEACHER'S NOTES FOR WEEK 6

DIGGING IN

1. In this passage, Paul addresses the question, "If God's grace abounds when we sin, why don't we keep on sinning so that God's grace would abound more?" In other words, if God extends free grace to us, forgiving our sins and granting us a righteous standing before him apart from anything good we do, doesn't that mean we can just live however we want?

2. Paul addresses this question because it is a sinner's natural response to hearing that God's grace abounds over our sin. When sinful people hear the good news of God's free forgiveness of sin through Christ, we instinctively want to twist that news in a way that gives us continued license to sin.

3. In this passage Paul says that all of the following have already happened to Christians:

- We've died to sin (v. 2).
- We were baptized into Christ's death (vv. 3–4).
- We have been united with Christ in a death like his (v. 5).
- Our old self was crucified with Christ (v. 6).
- We have been set free from sin (v. 7).
- We have been brought from death to life (v. 13).
- We are not under the power of the law but under grace (v. 14).

4. According to Paul, all these things have happened to us through our being united to Christ by faith.

5. In this passage Paul commands Christians to:

- Consider ourselves dead to sin but alive to God in Christ (v. 11).
- Not let sin reign in our bodies, to make us obey its passions (v. 12).
- Not present our bodies to sin as instruments for unrighteousness (v. 13).
- Present ourselves to God, and present our bodies to God as instruments for righteousness (v. 13).

6. The basic idea of verse 11 is that we are to *reckon* ourselves, *count* ourselves, *see* ourselves as dead to sin and alive to God. In other words, we are

to remind ourselves that because of our union with Christ we *are* dead to sin and alive to God.

7. In verse 14, Paul says that we are to present our members to God as instruments for righteousness, and not to sin as instruments of unrighteousness, because sin *will not have dominion over us*. That is, the power of sin in us has already been defeated through our union with Christ in his death and resurrection, and when we are glorified with Christ in the new earth, we will be free from sin forever.

8. That sin's power has already been defeated and that we will one day be perfectly free from sin is a great encouragement because it means that, since we are *not* under sin's power, we don't *need* to give in to it. In other words, Paul is saying that God has *enabled* us, through our union with Christ, by the Holy Spirit, to do what is pleasing in his sight.

9. Answers will vary, but the basic idea is that when we became Christians, we received not only a righteous status before God, but an entirely new self. So now, by God's grace, we are *able* to overcome sin and grow in holiness. Before we were Christians, we were living in sin and were dead to God, but now we're dead to sin and alive to God in Christ.

10. This passage teaches us that the gospel gives us a whole new self by which we are actually able to obey God. It also teaches that we grow in holiness by reflecting on, considering, and living in light of what God has already done for us in Christ. In other words, the gospel is what enables, empowers, and motivates our growth as Christians.

11. Paul's teaching differs from this common mode of instruction because instead of saying, "You are not [for example] pure, you should be pure, therefore be pure," he says, "You *are* dead to sin and alive to God in Christ, therefore *consider yourself* dead to sin and alive to God, and serve God instead of serving sin." In other words, Paul commands Christians to live in light of who they already are in Christ and in light of what God has already done for them in Christ.

12. Answers will vary, but the basic idea in each case is to encourage the person that they've died to their sinful nature, that sin no longer has dominion over them, that they now have new spiritual life in Christ, and so they are *able¸* by God's Spirit, to overcome that sin. In other words, rather than simply telling them what they should do, we should encourage such individuals with what God has already done for them in Christ and how the gospel has already freed them from bondage to their sin.

TEACHER'S NOTES FOR WEEK 7

DIGGING IN

1. In this passage Paul appeals to us based on the mercies of God.

2. This refers to God's grace in the gospel which Paul has just expounded for eleven chapters. Paul explains in these chapters that through the death and resurrection of Christ, God has forgiven our sins, given us a righteous standing before him, reconciled us to himself, given us new life and a new self in Christ, and revealed his gracious purposes toward us.

3. In verse 2, Paul tells us *not* to be conformed to this world. Instead, we are *to be* transformed *by* the renewal of our minds so that we may discern God's will.

4. Here are all the things Paul exhorts us to do in this passage, along with whether they are primarily individual or corporate.

Command	Individual or Corporate?
Don't think of yourself more highly than you ought, but think of yourself with sober judgment (v. 3).	Individual
Use the gifts God has given you to build up others (vv. 4-8).	Corporate
Love others genuinely (v. 9).	Corporate
Abhor what is evil and hold fast to what is good (v. 9).	Individual
Love one another with brotherly affection (v. 10).	Corporate
Outdo one another in showing honor (v. 10).	Corporate
Be fervent in spirit as you serve the Lord (v. 11).	Individual
Rejoice in hope, be patient in tribulation, and be constant in prayer (v. 12).	Individual
Contribute to the needs of the saints (v. 13).	Corporate
Seek to show hospitality (v. 13).	Corporate

5. The gospel equips us to think of ourselves with sober judgment because it reveals both the depth of our sin before God and the wonderful truth that in Christ, God has accepted us and declared us righteous. This frees us from

basing our standing before God on our good works, which means that we can frankly admit our sins, failures, and weaknesses.

6. One valid answer is: If we think of ourselves more highly than we ought to, we will be proud and arrogant toward others, selfishly using them to further our own agendas rather than seeking to serve them for our good. (Much more could be said here.)

7. If we think of ourselves with sober judgment, we will be more willing to bear with others and forgive their sins, knowing that God has forgiven us of much. We will also be more willing to humbly serve others instead of demanding that others serve us. (Much more could be said here.)

8. In light of our new status as members of the body of Christ, Paul exhorts us to use our gifts to build up others.

9. Answers will vary.

10. The gospel equips and motivates us to love and honor others in that:

- It frees us from slavery to self-love (Rom. 6:1–14).
- It demonstrates the greatness of God's love toward us (Rom. 5:6–8), which empowers us to love others.
- Through the gospel, God has showered us with undeserved honor, which should make us willing and eager to honor others.

11. As Christians, we have been the recipients of God's extraordinary, extravagant generosity in Christ. Therefore, the gospel enables us to give generously to others out of the overflow of what God has given to us. Rather than regarding our possessions as *ours*, we know that everything we have is from God. And since God has given us what we most need—salvation—at great cost to himself, we should be willing to provide others' needs, even when it costs us much.

12–14. Answers will vary.

9Marks

Building Healthy Churches

9Marks exists to equip church leaders with a biblical vision and practical resources for displaying God's glory to the nations through healthy churches.

To that end, we want to see churches characterized by these nine marks of health:

1 Expositional Preaching
2 Biblical Theology
3 A Biblical Understanding of the Gospel
4 A Biblical Understanding of Conversion
5 A Biblical Understanding of Evangelism
6 Biblical Church Membership
7 Biblical Church Discipline
8 Biblical Discipleship
9 Biblical Church Leadership

Find all our Crossway titles
and other resources at
www.9Marks.org

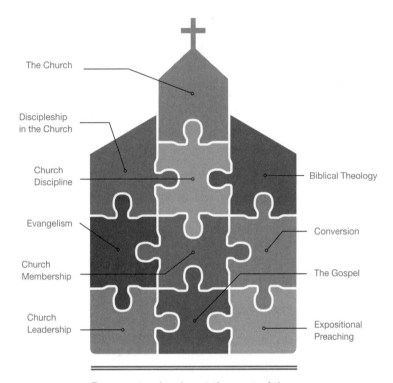

The Church

Discipleship
in the Church

Church
Discipline

Evangelism

Church
Membership

Church
Leadership

Biblical Theology

Conversion

The Gospel

Expositional
Preaching

Be sure to check out the rest of the
**9MARKS HEALTHY CHURCH
STUDY GUIDE SERIES**

This series covers the nine distinctives
of a healthy church as originally laid out
in *Nine Marks of a Healthy Church* by
Mark Dever. Each book explores the
biblical foundations of key aspects of
the church, helping Christians to live
out those realities as members of a
local body. A perfect resource for use in
Sunday school, church-wide studies, or
small group contexts.